Workman Kids • Workman Publishing • Hachette Book Group, Inc.
1290 Avenue of the Americas, New York, NY 10104 • workman.com

Workman Kids is an imprint of Workman Publishing, a division of Hachette Book Group, Inc. The Workman name and logo are registered trademarks of Hachette Book Group, Inc.

Design by Andrew Wang

The publisher is not responsible for websites (or their content) that are not owned by the publisher.

Workman books may be purchased in bulk for business, educational, or promotional use. For information, please contact your local bookseller or the Hachette Book Group Special Markets Department at special.markets@hbgusa.com.

Library of Congress Cataloging-in-Publication Data is available.

ISBN 978-1-5235-2993-3 • First Edition August 2025

Printed in Dongguan, China 08/25 APS

10 9 8 7 6 5 4 3 2

Hide-and-Seek
with Santa Claus

By Carolyn Fabris

Illustrated by Yen Abis

This Way to Grandma's

WORKMAN PUBLISHING
NEW YORK

"Grandma! Grandpa!" we shout.
"Is Santa here yet?"

"I think he's hiding . . . You'll find him, I bet!"

We start our seeking.
We look high and low.

Where could Santa be hiding?
We don't know!

He's not behind the tree.

Not under the bed.

He's not in the chimney,
or out by the sled.

He's not having cookies
and milk by the tree.

When we ask Grandma,
she says, "Don't ask me!"

We don't see the reindeer,
we can't find his sleigh.

Has he gone to the neighbors?

Or farther away?

Look! We see presents!

Santa must be near.

We found him! **Hooray!**
Our Santa is here!